CONTENTS

Fight for the cup 4

The Iberian Derby 10

Who wins the most? 16

Stars on the pitch 24

    Glossary 30

    Find out more 31

    Index 32

    About the author 32

Words in **bold** are in the glossary.

FIGHT FOR THE CUP

Portugal and Spain's men's national football teams faced off. It was the 2010 World Cup. They were playing for a spot in the quarter-finals. Portugal attacked hard in the first half. But they did not score. Neither did Spain.

Portugal and Spain have a football **rivalry**. The two countries are neighbours. Fans get excited about their matches.

WORLD CUP RIVALS

PORTUGAL
VS
SPAIN

by Jules Allen

a Capstone company — publishers for children

Raintree is an imprint of Capstone Global Library Limited, a company incorporated in England and Wales having its registered office at 264 Banbury Road, Oxford, OX2 7DY – Registered company number: 6695582

www.raintree.co.uk
myorders@raintree.co.uk

Copyright © Capstone Global Library Limited 2023

The moral rights of the proprietor have been asserted. All rights reserved. No part of this publication may be reproduced in any form or by any means (including photocopying or storing it in any medium by electronic means and whether or not transiently or incidentally to some other use of this publication) without the written permission of the copyright owner, except in accordance with the provisions of the Copyright, Designs and Patents Act 1988 or under the terms of a licence issued by the Copyright Licensing Agency, 5th Floor, Shackleton House, 4 Battle Bridge Lane, London, SE1 2HX (www.cla.co.uk). Applications for the copyright owner's written permission should be addressed to the publisher.

ISBN 978 1 3982 4858 8

Editorial Credits
Editor: Erika L. Shores; Designer: Dina Her; Media Researchers: Jo Miller and Pam Mitsakos; Production Specialist: Tori Abraham

Image Credits
Alamy: Allstar Picture Library Ltd, 6, Matt Dunham, 9, PA Images, 17, 19, REUTERS, 26; Associated Press: Armando Franca, 5; Getty Images: Andreas Rentz, 23, Bob Thomas/Popperfoto, 14; Shutterstock: ALEKSA2013, 10, Alizada Studios, 12, bamrung isarakul, Cover (players), D. Ribeiro, 13, Gevorg Ghazaryan, 29, Globe Turner, Cover (Portugal flag), Loveshop, Cover (Spain flag), Macrovector, Cover (arena), Oleg Batrak, 20, ph.FAB, 25, SPF, 11, tuulijumala, Cover (lights), vectorlaboratory, Cover, 1, (ball)

Design elements:
Shutterstock: huangyailah488, Ursa Major

All internet sites appearing in back matter were available and accurate when this book was sent to press.

British Library Cataloguing in Publication Data:
A full catalogue record for this book is available from the British Library.

Printed and bound in the United Kingdom

Spain's Xabi Alonso (red) and Portugal's Pedro Mendes (white)

Spain came on strong in the second half. In the 63rd minute they attacked. They ran the ball down the pitch. They used short passes.

Spain's player Xavi got the ball. He made a **backheel pass** out wide.

FACT

The World Cup happens every four years. Spain has played in it 15 times. Portugal has played in it seven times.

Spain's David Villa ran towards the goal. He received the pass. He took a quick shot on goal. Portugal's goalie blocked it.

The ball rolled back to Villa. Villa shot again. The ball flew into the back of the net. Goal! Neither team scored again. Spain won 1–0.

FACT
Spain later won the 2010 World Cup. They beat the Netherlands 1–0 in the final.

David Villa (on the right, in red) scores.

THE IBERIAN DERBY

Portugal and Spain make up the Iberian **Peninsula**. It is in south-west Europe. The rivalry is sometimes called the Iberian Derby.

Spain and Portugal have fought each other in wars. Spain invaded Portugal several times. Portugal is a much smaller country.

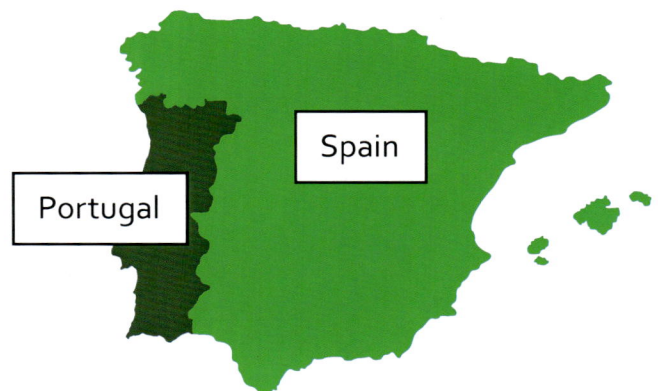

Spain and Portugal each have strong teams. They have played against each other for a long time. Spain has won many more of their matches.

Spain's national team in 2018

Portugal's national team in 2021

The two teams first played in 1921. Spain beat Portugal 3–1. It was a **friendly** match. These games are not official. Players use them to practise.

Spain (dark shirts) during a 1934 World Cup match

The first official match between the teams was in 1934. It was a World Cup **qualifying** game. Spain won 9–0. Spain made it to their first World Cup. They lost to Italy in the quarter-finals.

Six regions hold qualifying tournaments. The top teams earn a spot at the World Cup. Spain and Portugal are in the Europe region.

FACT

The Europe region has 55 teams. European teams have won the World Cup many times.

WHO WINS THE MOST?

Spain won or drew all their matches against Portugal for years. Portugal finally won in 1947. The great player Eusébio helped Portugal win more in the 1960s.

Eusébio

Portugal made it to the World Cup in 1966. They finished in third place. Eusébio scored four goals in the quarter-final game. He scored Portugal's only goal in the semi-finals. They lost 2–1 to England.

Portugal's Eusébio (left) and England's Nobby Stiles (right)

Spain's national team, 2012 Euros

Portugal and Spain play in the European Championship. It is often called the Euros.

The early 2000s were a great time for Spanish sports fans. Spain won the Euros in 2008. They won the World Cup in 2010. They won the Euros again in 2012.

Portugal became a stronger team from 2003. That's when Cristiano Ronaldo began playing for them. He is one of the best players ever.

In 2004, Portugal and Spain played at the Euros. Portugal won 1–0. It was the first time they had beaten Spain since 1981. Portugal made it to the final. They lost 1–0 to Greece.

Spain's Carles Puyol (left) and Ronaldo (right) in 2004

STARS ON THE PITCH

Both teams have had many star players. Ronaldo helped Portugal finish fourth at the 2006 World Cup.

Ronaldo has played well at the Euros. He helped Portugal win Euro 2016. In 2021, Ronaldo scored five goals at the tournament.

FACT
Ronaldo has scored more goals in international matches than any other male player.

Andrés Iniesta

Andrés Iniesta is one of the best Spanish players ever. He helped Spain win the Euros in 2008 and 2012.

Iniesta was the hero of the 2010 World Cup final. Spain played the Netherlands. Four minutes were left in extra time. Iniesta received a pass and scored. Spain won 1–0.

FACT
At Euro 2012, Iniesta was named Player of the Tournament.

In 2018, Spain and Portugal met at the World Cup. They played in an early round. Ronaldo scored three goals. The match ended 3–3.

The two teams have become more evenly matched. Fans and players care a lot about the rivalry. They look forward to exciting games in the future.

GLOSSARY

backheel pass when a player uses the back of the foot to pass the ball to a teammate behind them

friendly in football, a game that does not count towards a tournament

peninsula a piece of land with water on three sides

qualifying a stage in which competitors try to win entry into an event

rivalry a fierce feeling of competition between two groups over a long period of time

FIND OUT MORE

BOOKS

FIFA World Cup 2022 Kids' Handbook, Kevin Pettman (Welbeck Children's Books, 2022)

The Unofficial Guide to the World Cup, Paul Mason (Franklin Watts, 2022)

What You Never Knew About Cristiano Ronaldo, Martha E. H. Rustad (Raintree, 2023)

WEBSITES

European Qualifiers: Portugal
uefa.com/european-qualifiers/teams/110--portugal/

FIFA World Cup Facts for Kids
kids.kiddle.co/FIFA_World_Cup

Spain National Football Team Facts for Kids
kids.kiddle.co/Spain_national_football_team

INDEX

1966 World Cup 18
2006 World Cup 24
2010 World Cup 4, 8, 21, 27
2018 World Cup 28

European Championship (Euros)
   21, 22, 24, 27
Eusébio 16, 18

fans 4, 28
friendlies 13

Iberian Derby 10
Iniesta, Andrés 27

qualifying tournaments 15
quarter-finals 4, 15, 18

Ronaldo, Cristiano 22, 24, 28

Villa, David 8

wars 10

Xavi 7

ABOUT THE AUTHOR

Jules Allen is a children's book editor and author. She loves sports, art, all kinds of books and small dogs.